Books by Richard Howard

Poetry

NO TRAVELLER   *1989*

LINING UP   *1983*

MISGIVINGS   *1979*

FELLOW FEELINGS   *1976*

TWO-PART INVENTIONS   *1974*

FINDINGS   *1971*

UNTITLED SUBJECTS   *1969*

THE DAMAGES   *1967*

QUANTITIES *1962*

Criticism

ALONE WITH AMERICA   *1969*
EXPANDED EDITION   *1980*

PREFERENCES   *1974*

No Traveller

NO TRAVELLER

Poems by **Richard Howard**

New York *Alfred A. Knopf* *1989*

THIS IS A BORZOI BOOK
PUBLISHED BY ALFRED A. KNOPF, INC.

Poems in this book were originally published as follows:

Even in Paris: SALMAGUNDI
Triangulations: POETRY
Famed Dancer Dies of Phosphorus Poisoning: POETRY
Love Which Alters: GRAND STREET
A Sorceror's Apprentice: GRAND STREET
. . .Always With You: CINCINNATI POETRY REVIEW
The Foreigner Remembered by a Local Man, copyright © 1987 by Richard Howard. Reprinted from FOR NELSON MANDELA, edited by Jacques Derrida and Mustapha Tlili, published by Seaver Books / Henry Holt and Company, 1987.
Mademoiselle's Last Sunday: THE NATION
Concerning K: THE NEW YORKER
Stanzas in Bloomsbury: THE PARIS REVIEW
Colored Stones: THE YALE REVIEW
Oracles: GRAND STREET

Library of Congress Cataloging-in-Publication Data

Howard, Richard, 1929–
    No traveller.

    I. Title.
PS3558.08826N6   1989   811'.54   88–45799
ISBN 0–394–57466–4
ISBN 0–394–72302–1 (pbk.)

Manufactured in the United States of America
First Edition

for David Alexander

withal

I

EVEN IN PARIS   3

I I

TRIANGULATIONS   33

FAMED DANCER DIES OF PHOSPHORUS
   POISONING   39

LOVE WHICH ALTERS   42

A SORCERER'S APPRENTICE   46

. . .ALWAYS WITH YOU   52

THE FOREIGNER REMEMBERED BY A
   LOCAL MAN   55

MADEMOISELLE'S LAST SUNDAY   57

CONCERNING K   60

STANZAS IN BLOOMSBURY   63

COLORED STONES   65

I I I

ORACLES   71

(I)

EVEN IN PARIS

TO THE MEMORY OF
L. DONALD MAHER
(1921–1966)

(I)

Dear Roderick,
you are repeatedly missed,
and it is a poor, *showy* charity
on your part to leave us for . . . Schenectady:
I trust your Ma has been made
properly conscious of the sacrifice!
How long will it be till you can bring yourself
back to our selfish Paris?
Until you do, I suppose I had better
keep you filled in—an expression no Frenchman
would be caught dead (or alive)
employing. But what else are letters for?
I think the French are afraid of anything
full or filling: to them
pleine is pregnant (*ergo* French letters, love) . . .
Not "filled in"—I'll keep you *au courant* instead:
fallow still, and French as well!

Well then, the day after your departure,
one of those dark mornings only Paris knows
how to drop in December
like a swine before pearls, I got up
(one must always get up) and in your absence
determined to dedicate
myself to seasonable good works:
indeed I found my old *doyenne* stowed away
just where you said she would be,
bundled up like a bagful of knitting
in the Rue Jacob pavillion. Quite macabre . . .
"Miss Barney! Dear Miss Barney!"

3

Even in Paris

I shouted through layers of lilac sheets,
lace shawls, peignoir, bonnet, scarves, Lord knows what else,
    but she—*l'Amazone*! Miss Boss!
    lordliest lesbian in the Faubourg
    (that was at least half a century ago
        and a whole *cénacle*,
    which seems, once more, to have followed her lead
into oblivion), Nathalie Clifford Barney!—
    smiling her goat's smile, murmured
    in a thrilling baritone that *talking*
was no use: "I am altogether deaf now—
    such a comfort. I have found
    words much nicer since they make no sound."
I bustled and fussed round her *filthy* bolster
    —what was the concierge *doing*?—
and dropped my questionnaire under the lamp
beside her teeth. Armed with that set of choppers
    (soaking in what—*sauternes*?)
    she could certainly contend with a few
prompted *souvenirs*. No need for me. I fled.

    Opportunely, it turned out:
    remember those tickets you gave me for
the *concert spirituel* in Sainte Chapelle?
    Richard was *lurking* inside:
    "Must be the first time in five-hundred years,"
he whispered, "the monument is being used
        for a music hall: Poulenc!"
    Volleys of coughing ensued (December
in Paris: I am sure you still recollect
    the likelihood of *la grippe*
    in those great stone barns—*ex cathedra* chills!)
but while we waited, a sudden winter sun,
    clearly bored with Catholic
    festivals—Christmas especially,
which is only for servants—dim, dull, divine,

4

changed the chapel to glory,
the entire west wall luminous—alive.
All at once, sitting there, bald Richard began
staring (across me) at this
fat man under the windows, red or blue
as the famished light devoured the famous glass . . .
He might have had anybody's
face—absolutely unremarkable,
as though he had been obliged to put up with
something ready-made until
more suitable features could be made
to order—and since the proper article
had never been delivered,
he had gone about in this blank disguise
the greater part of his life! Richard went on
peering at . . . what? What appeared
matter-of-factness at the expense of
matter *and* of fact. Splendor crept over
our row until it covered
even Monsieur X with medieval grace—
Rod, you'll never guess! He fell on his knees,
arms out, as if receiving
stigmata from stained glass! And then got up
as if nothing had occurred, dusting his pants
and muttering (Richard heard),
"A little kneeling is a dangerous thing."
Which served, it would seem, as a sort of password:
over my red body, our
Richard (who as you would say does believe
in taking the bull by the udders) began
whispering questions—In French
at first (and you know what his French is like—
like worms on the lawn, coming in and out) and
the fat man answering as if
the language had sinned and he was assigned
to punish it, then switching (both) to English

with an evident relief,
murmuring relentlessly away. But
then the music started—all I made out was:
"... an attempt to escape self
is likely to be identical with
an attempt to discover it ..." Whereupon
the *Stabat Mater* "filled in"
(how else to put it? I was as nearly
bored as enthusiasm would permit), yet the scene
instead of being cut short
as it should, went on, Richard *obbligato,*
hissing interrogations in that way he has
of answering them himself:
"How do you find Paris, from inside, I mean—
wonderfully homogeneous, don't you think?
Have you met French people here?"
and even (you know Richard) "Is *your* French
adequate to your needs? Might I be of help?"
I can't tell if Richard is
very forward or just very backward,
but when this person actually *did* reply:
"The French conceal their virtues
and flaunt all their vices on the surface;
ludicrous, I call it, their lust for dragging
everything into the light"—
Richard looked as if he had just been slapped.
Or kissed. And just then, nicely framing the scene,
the sun forsook the windows,
and the whole damned Sainte Chapelle turned to *merde:*
nothing so dead as stained glass lit from inside.
Richard, *of course*, persisted
with his nonsense about the *unity*
of Paris ... And lurching past, this person left
with Richard hanging on his words:
"The French always believe equality
consists in cutting off what sticks out ..."

My dear!
Now Roderick, according
to Richard, our *anonimo* was none
other than the Fourteenth Way of Looking at
a Bleak Bard—R claims he knows
the face (incredible!): Why don't you do
a touch of detective work for me . . . Granted
there was something of the priest
in the man, or perhaps of the eunuch . . .
Who knows? Richness, ripeness, even just a touch
of rottenness . . . "My poet in Paris!"
Richard kept harping, "who means more to me
than all your harridans ever could to you . . .
So I did, in fact, see Shelley
plain, even in Paris." "Very plain," said I,
which released a salvo of salacity
about my "Sapphic goose-girls,
Romaine, Rachilde, and Ida Rubenstein! . . ."
This argued with all the eager energy
whereby he overpowers
even the people who agree with him!
Do find out for me—just for fun—if this poet
Richard has such designs on
is still in Connecticut . . . or is here,
after all? Can it matter, such a *creature's*
being on hand—even on foot?

Meanwhile I managed to grope my way
through the disconsolations of a Paris
twilight, across the river
and into the *boîte*, sniffling all the way
to the dear Reine Blanche, a menagerie
without cages, and the night
closed down as usual. Who cares whom we meet
by day—it's what we do in the dark that's real!
All I ask is for someone

7

to make me fervent, and I'll do his
bedding. Remember? Happy New Year,

IVO

(II)

DEAR RODERICK, the New Year has set in—
like an epidemic. The wolves are gone,
but Villon has the winter down *patte-bas*!

Christmas *is* a deadly season here,
illustrating the old Parisian rule:
every silver lining is tarnished by clouds.

Life seems so piecemeal: "Oh that, that belongs
to my Litter Period." So much for '52.
Perhaps just sending this, or anything,

to Schenectady will make the pieces fit.
News—not mine, but *the* news, Roderick,
leaves me at a loss for language, clogged

like a bottle of Burgundy held upside down.
Guess what! Paris is being visited
(*graced* is hardly the word) by Crispin himself!

who never once in seventy years detoured
farther out of territorial
waters than a weekend in Key West.

Remember Edna's story about Henry James
preferring to stay among the vegetables
when she took him with her to Les Halles—

"precisely because their organs of increase
are not so prominent." . . . Was Europe's meat
too bloody for my poet all these years?

Yet there he sat, the old Comedian,
continuous as an eggshell, right beside
Ivo, and freezing like the rest of us

—only from higher motives, I am sure—
in Sainte Chapelle, contingency resolved
to kingliness. Each time I tried to make

acknowledgments, the Poulenc interfered,
as well as Ivo's scowling all the while,
like a Dying Swan that is very, very cross.

"The kings sit down to music, and the queens"
—to alter Kipling's verse—"stand up to dance,"
by which I mean that Ivo ran away

once I informed him who our neighbor was . . .
Another *fine*, another *fin-de-siècle*
feast or fast with dying dowagers:

the past is always Ivo's choice because
it is drained of fear. I braved the present out,
putting the usual impertinences as

to When and Where and Does the prospect please,
and Will you go on to visit Italy?
("I think not. Italians are only the French

in a good mood.") At least I got replies!
"The tourist's purpose is to be delighted.
Nothing odd or obscure. I have survived

too long on postcards from Paris or Toulon.
At my age, I may say, life melts in the hand,
and I have dined enough with the faithful dead."

Timid yet tenacious, I asked on—
they must have been the questions he could use;
he did not turn away, yet seemed to exude

a gentleness no longer incarnate but somehow
hovering above him in a nimbus, even though
the light in Sainte Chapelle was going dim . . .

Roderick, I was gossiping with a god!
Maybe because I showed I knew as much
without an autograph or a lock of hair,

I was told I might escort him—*steer*, he said—
to the Louvre next day. ("What I want to see
is in the Orangery: is that the Louvre too?")

in order to make "sense" of the *Nymphéas* . . .
"I have been told one is embraced, they curve
around one in a continuous ecstasy . . .

It seems worth leaving even Hartford for that.
I have always wanted to stand inside the light
which falls at home—falls out, falls down: falls,

that is the point. In Hartford, the light falls,
and what is fallen does not cease to fall.
I'd like to let those water-lilies have

their way with me; I'd like to learn from them:
if anything could be explained, then everything
would be explained . . ." There was, of course, a catch!

No one's to know he ever came here—no
first impressions of Paris, photographs
of boulevard encounters, above all

no poems. The whole preposterous episode
is to be wiped out, elided—*never was!*
I made a stab: "And have you come with Mrs. . . ?"

"No. Journeys taken together lead to hell.
I want to be, this once, a living man
and a posthumous artist. Ideal. Shall we, then?"

Surely this was He-Mannerism at its best,
an invitation being the sincerest form
of flattery; besides, it was a mere *traipse*

squiring the old absquatulator home
to his safe haven in—where else?—the Ritz!
Even incognito our Crispin knows his place.

We talked, or he—dialogue being no more
than a literary fiction taken for a fact
of life—*he* talked, in a timbre bearing words

before him on a salver: "Limelight is bad.
What's best for me is half-light . . . *crépuscule?*
La lumière qui tombe entre deux tabourets:

the profit of French is how readily it submits
to prose. I suppose I am one of those [three rhymes!]
who can tell you at dusk what others deny by day."

By now we had advanced to the Place Vendôme
where the Column bedevils what it can't adorn
and where, at the wicked doorway of the Ritz,

the din of inequity swallowed up my man
as if there were no such still pond as poets!
The night remained. How sad it is to part

from people we've known only a little while!
Hours to pass, to pass through, to pass by. . .
I stopped at the Reine. Ivo of course had flown

that brazen coop which would display till dawn
a nature shocking-pink in tooth and claw. . .
Not much rest tonight. The rest anon.

*   *   *

Well, dear, we reached the *empty* Orangerie
(day-after-Christmas void) and there we stood,
enveloped by the ovals of nenuphars

—yes, rather *like* the islands of Langerhans,
actually: there *is* an anatomical sense
of visceral perspectives. Once inside,

you must admit, a cycle of mustard and mauve
makes it hard to link how much there is *of* it
to how little there is *to* it. Roderick,

do you know what a *temenos* is? A ring of dread,
the invulnerable range the Greeks proposed
around their gods and heroes. That's what I saw:

my poet paralyzed by the perimeter
of a wave without horizon, without shore. . .
He stood stock still, and I think it was awe

he felt at how the visual could turn
visionary. He stayed there a long while
(I, meantime, loaded up on postcards: X

marks where he stood, admonished by Monet.)
"We also ascend dazzling," is all he said,
or all I could make out—is it a quote?

You'd have thought I had *awakened* him
by shouting in his ear; he started up
when I *whispered* was he happy? "Happy here?

—how hideous the happiness one wants,
how beautiful the misery one has! . . .
I think I'll stay a little longer here.

Alone." I left him then, of course—
mine was the backward glance of Orpheus
or of Lot's Wife, the unretarding gaze

that loses the beloved where last seen:
my Sacred Monster loomed, one big black lump
in a circle of besieging light, and Rod,

he was slowly, in a sort of demonic shuffle,
turning, turning round the oval room,
palms out and humming harshly to himself—

it was, I could tell, a ritual exploit
danced by the world's most deliberate dervish—not
whirling but centripetal. Outside

the air was crumbling, there was no more sky—
only that Paris substitute which fills
the calendar till spring. Ivo won't know

what he incanted like a sacred text:
"We also ascend dazzling." All Ivo knows
is Rumanian nursery rhymes and the Almanach

da Gotha, which he keeps in his medicine chest.
Roderick, do you recognize the phrase?
Myself I think—however insane I may be—

it does console one to have living gods
on whose warm altars one can lay one's wreath,
as I have done—I brought him there, after all.

Dear Roderick, if you have been denied
such aptitudes of worship, I pity you.
But enough about you, dear, let me return

to my distances, my deference: the great
are like high mountains, you must be
away from them to enjoy them properly.

I'd better stop before I've told it all—
some people can tell all before they start;
suppose you try, dear.
                              Happy New Year.

                    R I C H A R D

(III)

EPIPHANY.

Today's red letters, Roderick,
in my new Hermès *carnet*
are entirely apposite to last night;
the Great Event, on which my various wiles
converged, has ultimately . . .
eventuated, and I am at peace,
though as you apprehended, out of pocket:
one does not dine with a duke
or even a diva and get off cheap.
It can best be reckoned, my affecting *fête*,
as a conjugation of
irregular verbs: I disbursed, she gorged,
he dozed, we guzzled, and they—down to the last
garçon at the Tour d'Argent—
they cleaned up. By now the party has
that incontrovertible inevitability
always ascribed to the past.
None of it was easy—recall the cast:
the royals, the Count, Romaine resuscitated
and Zinka semi-extinct. . .
The arduous part had been to get Romaine
out of bed (she never sleeps, but lives and moves
and has her belongings there)
and into more—or less—than a tuxedo.
Z was wearing some beautiful old Lalique
that seemed, on her, oddly placed—
like bits of Palestrina rendered by
the dinner orchestra. Of course we set out,
for Zinka's sake, in French
but I get up hungry from French (not from

the Tour d'Argent: *canard pressé* answers to
    all my unhurried longings) . . .
  Besides, as soon as she was satisfied
we had paid sufficient attention to her,
    Zinka lapsed cheerfully
    into her *asperges blanches truffées*,
and we were in English, if not at ease. Rod,
    do you remember those *chairs?*
  Cushions so thickly covered with buttons
that one feels like a very sensitive bun
    having its raisins put in!
  I can't think how "David" (please to observe
the ease with which the Duke's name leaps from my lips)
    contrives to sleep so soundly
    on such upholstery. I sat across,
noticing how his hair has turned so much lighter,
    his wrinkles so much darker
    in the Nassau sun, that he seems to be
a negative of himself. He gives the feel,
    even the smell, of decay,
    of aristocracy *in extremis,*
sinister and trivial and gentle and strange—
    just like an exquisite goat.
  Romaine ignored the tiny snores and launched
across the lobster Newburgh ("a nice *purée,*"
    the Count had just confided,
    "of white kid gloves") into that old routine,
her dissection of Duff Cooper: "the only
    ambassador whose portrait
  I was *embarrassed* to paint—it was not
that his *derrière* was so much bigger than mine,
    but that his teeth, when he smiled,
    came in three colors: yellow, blue and black!
Excruciating sittings—he *would* smile. And dull . . ."
    Whereat the Duchess chimed in,
    abounding in her sense: "*Harold* once said

Duff had been offered thirty thousand pounds
        to bore the Channel Tunnel."
    it seemed to bring her back to life—
though it is one thing to be admired because
        you are so attractive, and
    quite another to be admired because
you are so attractive still. She really was
        smothered, or at least choked,
    in rubies ("four days of a fish diet
and you can wear anything, my dear"), and while
        Romaine's own teeth rattled on
    like dice in a box, the Duchess advanced
to Lady Diana. . . "To hear her talk, *as she does*,
        about her escape from France,
    you would suppose she had swum the Channel
with her maid between her teeth!" And in the noise
        of sudden silence that fell,
    a kind of ghastly horticultural calm,
the Duke appeared to have wakened—to have *heard:*
        "Really, Wallis! there are times
    when I fear your taste is . . . elementary."
Roderick, he started up and spoke her name
        with so sharp an emphasis
    that a man at the table nearest ours
whirled round as if someone had been calling roll
        —as if he had been found out!
    And you know, I am sure he was the one
Richard *attached* himself to at Sainte Chapelle,
        munching alone now, as if
    on both sides of the Communion Table,
a sort of solitary manducation *de luxe!*
        Of course I asked all around
    if anyone knew who "that gentleman" was,
but to no avail. How much of a lion can he be?
        I may take no exercise
    except jumping to conclusions, but who

wants to believe "my great poet" looks like that—
    an apathetic mushroom
  in gray flannel whom you could no more
read than you could stab a pillow to the heart!
    Zinka, meanwhile, just like all
  deaf people, was provoked because the Count
—so kind!—was repeating Wallis's remark
    which she had happened to hear . . .
The Duchess turned, contrite, to her Duke
and vowed to spend next week in mourning—"except
    for stockings: I haven't worn
  black stockings since I gave up the can-can."
By then Romaine, who enjoys a joke, so long
    as the point is obvious,
  had managed to modify her molars
to match the *mousse au mocha* and seemed eager
    to regain what she regarded
  as due dominance of the table by
describing "my first encounter with your dad"
    —this to the Duke of Windsor!—
"at which I do recall a remark made,
one which struck me at the time as notably
    happy, but unhappily
  a remark made by me, and not by His
Majesty." Even the Duke actually laughed
    aloud—a likely signal
  for table-talk to dwindle down to pairs,
which in our circumstances, given our set,
    meant that in every instance
  of utterance, it was only one step
from the incredible to the indispensable.
    As the sole participant
  with perfect hearing, I am empowered
to report one provocative moment when
    the Count, trumpeting into
  Zinka's better ear, announced that he liked

nothing more than lying on his bed an hour
    with his favorite Trollope!
  (but in a circle such as ours, of course,
not much interest was taken, either way)...
    Still, I am fond of my *fête*,
  and when you moralize: *où sont les neiges*,
or rather: where is the cracked ice of yesteryear?
    I shall always remember
  not so much the unforgettable group
(one soon forgets the merely unforgettable)
    as that sad, fat diner
  turning with real terror in his face
when David shouted Wallis's name... Was he not
    just *there*, like an accident
  looking for somewhere to happen?
                 Roderick,
if I were you, I shouldn't hold my shutter
    open in Connecticut:
  I think Richard must be right, and the Blue
Guitarist *was* among us. What is the use
    of lying when the truth, well-
  distributed, serves the same purpose?
Perhaps he'll attend my next *petit souper*,
    assuming I can persuade
  him to come or Richard to escort him:
hard to determine what the lesser evil is...
    Meanwhile Paris must survive
  the rest of January and therefore
the punishing presence of the commonplace:
    other people's lives remain
  decorative, to all appearances,
only provided one takes no part in them.
    Enjoy Schenectady, dear,
  and give my love to your Ma, if she can
use it. I see I am running out of news:
    better to dry up than dribble...

Nothing but silence, then, and darkness in
la ville lumière: you deserve better from

I V O

(I V)

R O D E R I C K   D E A R, today was to be the last
my poet would spend in Paris—although *spending*
is hardly the verb for what I've hauled him through.

He's always praying life not to give him more
than what it can take back, "my poet" by right
of the cicerone's function, which has proved

a fitful pleasure but a constant joy:
he has that scrap of innocence which keeps
most of us from becoming such a bore,

though in his case there are astonishments:
his modernity seems to me miraculous,
as if he had already attended a party

—say, one of Ivo's ruinous *soirées*—
that has not yet been given. We have gone
to the Luxembourg, where Rilke said he had

buried his best bones; to the Palais-Royal,
counting which cornice had to be Colette's;
and ambled through the Comédie's arcades,

stopping at statues—"which *may* be dignified,
but the absence of which is *always* dignified:
extend to feeling and you have the dignity

of Symbolism." We have seen the Place des Vosges
—"grim, yes, apodictically grim,
but a grimness that has a way of looking pink. . .

Hugo's house? No. Better to think of him
back there on Guernsey. Or Jersey. Was it both?
Easier to endure his claptrap out of fog. . ."

You could see a justice in it, for just then
the sun came out and took a cloud or two
to do some high-class, grand-scale modelling,

Poussin, Puvis, all along the rooftops.
This whole day we scoured the capital,
soaking up the Tuileries, glaring in rows

over the sombre well of the Invalides,
after the pleasant Gallic fashion. Paris is
"beyond measure interesting." The point is,

he is never disappointed, though outraged
deeply enough to satisfy my own
resentment of these people and their past;

perambulating the quays, not long before
I took him to the Aerogare, he gave
the last of his Lutetian homilies,

the consequence of his holding off so long:
"I can't help it. What is more I don't
want to help it. I've reached a time of life

when nothing helps now; for me the word *France*
evokes a notion of courtesy, of the correct
pitch between persons, whereas the word *French*

means only a sullen concierge and disputes
in shops, alarmed pedestrians and rude
bus-drivers. All my life the word *France*

has meant unity and justice, while this week
I have learned to listen, in the word *French*
for the nuances of division, nepotism, shame. . .

Now I have seen the Louvre, where the word *France*
glorifies the idea of conscientious work,
art and organization, finished craft;

but among art dealers I find the word *French*
evokes the mystique of improvisation, no more
than a paltry and urbane expedience. . .

I have seen Notre Dame, and the word *France*
means a people standing above pettiness;
I have bought newspapers, and the word *French*

suggests a citizen never free from scandal—
and if he has done vile things, I am not
solaced by learning he quite meant to do them. . ."

We had reached the best of the bookstalls, the one
where you can find all the old Symbolistes;
I pointed out the complete *Mercure de France*,

year after yellow year. He opened one to find
—1897—the Bazalgette translation
of *Leaves of Grass: "Nous autres, nous montons*

éclatants et énormes, comme le soleil!
He quite intoned the words, as if the light
of January and the sudden wrack of cloud

that darkened the whole Seine were adequate
illumination: "Yes, but if the light
in your body be darkness, how great is darkness?"

The river moved, and we moved too—the books
in their iron boxes seemed to move with us,
literature from stall to stall the same,

most of the wretched tomes the color of mud,
of the sluggish river. He didn't seem to mind
the weather or the smudged, identical dross:

"The future of the past is never sure.
This must be the one place in the world
where a man can realize what he writes

is a river too. It is continuous,
no burden on the memory, but a way
—made up of all ways—of reaching the sea."

Rod, I shall never pass those dusty bins
and the hags who guard them (themselves guarded by
a shivering mongrel in a shabby quilt

eager to snap, the instant you reach in
for an uncut first of *Les Nourritures terrestres*)
without seeing him still above the river

—the river of books and the winter-weary Seine,
apparently quite content to let them both
run by him—to be *overrun* by what he sees. . .

He says the body forgets nothing, and reveres
things that do not return—for him no moment
is wholly lost: all past experience

is potentially present for him, and this one
visit can withstand an entire life!
He even responds to what seems singular:

three white swans paddling past the Louvre,
a copy of Pierre Louÿs's *Astarte*
(I got it for Ivo) that had once belonged

to Duse, according to the paraphed *dédicace*.
Everything "once belonged". All ownership
is a weakness which passes perception, as I learned:

abruptly he turned back to the *boîte* and bought
—without a cavil at the cost—that one
Whitman-honored volume of the *Mercure*

and stood with it at the top of the river stairs
like a rueful Père Noël, extending the book
and a fistful of hundred-franc notes as well!

to every passer-by, muttering his phrase,
"*lancer ce livre comme un bateau*", until
one boy stopped, snatched the money, plunged

unquestioningly down the slippery steps
(where every *clochard* in Paris must have pissed)
to the river itself, and leaning on a ring

set in the embankment launched the book
as if it were a Hindu barge—the waves
took it, open, floating, sinking. . . Whereupon

we drifted loose, neither of us speaking again
once my poet pronounced himself content—
"a ceremony bought is a ceremony still"

—walking single-file up the Rue des Saints-Pères
to the comparative safety of a *café-crème*.
Of course, once we left the river, I recalled

that what he had murmured in the Orangerie
was what he had found, in French, along the Seine.
I looked it up as soon as he had gone,

and I think I understand, now, why he stood
that way, revolving among the *Nymphéas:*
"How quick the sunrise would kill me," Whitman said,

"if I could not now and always send
sunrise out of me." It was the play
of surfaces that held him, infinite,

centerless, unstructured: only ecstasy,
an airless moment when he might not send
the water-lilies back. "Speech is the twin

of my vision . . . unequal to measure itself."
A moment there, he trembled on the brink
of what Sir Thomas Browne so grandly calls

"ingression into the divine shadow." But then
my old wizard—Wallace this time, not Walt—
summoned up his forces, mustered his magic,

and managed to meet Monet's with that same strength
he has survived by at home, where certainly
he differs from all poets since Eden who

in search of the invisible have obscured
the visible. Not surprising that his last
tourist touch should be to *see* something:

"Objects, other lives, inveterately appeal—
call to me, whether I answer them or not.
Would it be a nuisance to stop by

the bird-market behind the Hôtel-Dieu?
Toucans and tanagers, birds-of-paradise—
even time, perhaps, for a blue macaw;

nightingales are splendid creatures, if
only I had a bush that might afford
the right retreat. . ." Ivo had been warned

and with his latest *objet de vitrine*
posted to meet us at the Café de Flore.
Once I deliver my poet to the air

we can resume our halfway-decent lives.
Closing in, the day dies out in one's arms
at this hour, stretching its final light

in what would seem a final agony,
too proud to make more of a commotion
than that one patch purple to the left,

and up there, all that leaking peach.
You've seen cats die like that, haven't you?
stiffening into darkness without a sound. . .

Later my poet joined us at the Flore
where people listen to each other's alibis,
in what will be a *monologue des morts*:

once he leaves, we shall not hear of him,
only read his new book, his latest, his last.
It has been a week, Rod. Who would have thought

there was so much to learn about the moderns?
He is, or conceals, a very ancient myth,
and tending him is the arduous pursuit

of Ariel. From which only lust and tenderness
bring relief: a bird in the bush is worth
a feather in your cap. Love,

PAPAGENO

(V)

RODERICK DEAR, it is the last infirmity
        of illustrious clichés
    to be "deeply serious": I risk it
for the truth—truth is what I can't help thinking,
        and obliges me to ask
    what are poets for?
                Last night, Richard brought
his to our table—the stout fellow observed
    by the half-light of stained glass
and the full glare of Money's Tower, one
and the same corpulent anonymity,
        all introductions to whom
    were carefully fudged and camouflaged
by the heartiest kind of manly greetings—
        I prefer kissing people,
    handshakes are abhorrent, though I grant you:

desire distracts. No danger there—or here;
    the old gentleman had come
    fresh from the bird-market, which was to be
his final impression of Paris. Not bad.
      Only shyness made him seem
    a touch insolent. Intrinsically
his voice was elegiac, and I can't say
      that he had the vanity
    of the true artist: a serious reason
against his being one. He was stuffed so full
      of his avian *trouvailles*—
"Wings have been plucked from birds to make angels
of men, and claws from birds to make them devils"—
      there was no talking *to* him.
    Listening was odd enough, caviare
to the general, tripe to the few, something
      for everyone. He kept on
    about what he had evidently drunk
too much to keep to himself: "Just consider
      the neglected incidence
    of love-cries, the human phenomenon
hardly examined by any novelist,
      yet ranging as birdcalls do
    from whispers to the screech of hysteria,
always sounding alien to the emitter
      invaded and possessed by
    some astral spirit with wild ideas
of its own. . . The most mesmeric music I know,
      though literature is silent
    on the subject. It is the woefullest
ill of old age to be certain that one shall
      never hear a new version. . .
    Venturing along the rows of cages,
I heard them summoning me once again, birds
      or women—cadence itself
    at a certain pitch of intensity

becoming a form of substance. . ."

                                                Roderick,
        I may embroider somewhat—
    this is not all he textually said,
but what an enemy might be paid to quote
        from his words. I embellish,
    and you may detect a certain garlic
of derision in the salad I toss you
        (if your taste-buds have blossomed)
    —I could not endure another moment
of our complicitous little ritual:
        not Richard's adulation
    nor the presumptive poet's eruption.
His phoenix played the incendiary with
        all too manifest a faith
    in its own ashes. If you ask me, Rod,
the question of identity is still open.
        I grant you, he kept us all
    allured (and aloof), shining on us yet
hiding his light, like some great variable
        yet constant moon, *Somebody*!
But there is no bore like a brilliant bore,
and I believe Richard lost his way looking
        for a genius who might fuse
    life and art—*I* had abounding proof
that such a prodigy was not to be found—
        the formula still unknown.
    Richard, of course, with his love of poets
second only to his love of vulgarity
        would revel in the humbug—
    one more fly in the amber of homage.
Well, all of us long to have our Great Men—or,
        if we have something in us
    of a woman, we do like that something
to be a Great Lady. If we do not have
        Great Men or Ladies either,

we invent them. Myself I shall return
to my helpless monsters, nourishing for them
    a passion of finality. . .
Before I frequented my dear grand freaks
I ached and tried to turn away from the old—
    I feared how bored they must be,
    how listless and dispirited. I judge
differently now: they are reduced to *mere*
    existence, and do not mind!
Meanwhile I am sure R is writing too—
soon you will have other evidence by which
    to determine. . . Remember,
Hölderlin was a madman who refused
to believe he was Hölderlin. . . Here we do
    everything but anything,
    and I abandon Richard to his fate,
wishing him luck!. . . God created luck because
    He did not know what to do
    otherwise with those of us who cannot
make something out of ourselves.

                      Love ever,

                          I V O

(II)

Triangulations

1

Months of mute resentment, and *now* you mail
scenes from the life of a happily-married hunk,
kodachromes of the barn, puppies, the pool

much obscured by larkspur, poppies, banks
of lemon verbena. Postmarked EDENVILLE
and overlooked by Mt Adam *and* Mt Eve:

". . . acres of garden and notwithstanding snakes
we plant new hybrids every chance we get."
I thought one snake was all there had to be.

Yet oddly painless, after the primal shock,
to make you out, beside the compost heap,
in a pose of self-parody (it must be that)

so cunning and so pitiless—the way
you concentrate just inches wide of the lens
and smile as if you kept all promises—

it becomes auto-erotic, as I'm sure you know.
The scarf you always wore (one of the ones
I gave you, monster—have you no shame at all?)

dangles into your saluki's bedroom eyes:
each of you has too much long hair, a self-
indulgence irreproachable at this range,

and your hand in your pocket seems to intimate
practices once perfected. Still, no pain,
truly, not the faintest covetous twinge—

i.e., the real estrangement has occurred,
the kind which no longer causes suffering.
Is that foxglove? all that purple blur,

or heliotrope? I can almost hear the bees;
and that, I assume, is your Elizabeth
—a pretty girl is like an allergy—

sitting pretty in the middle of the bed.
Or is it elegy? I trust she knows
the bad old days are always somebody's *belle*

époque, and that body happened to be mine. . .
So now you do Movements, Sacred Dances, Leaps
into Labor: I can listen to what you do

because I don't have to remember what you did.
The whole scene smacks of the doll's house, in the pre-
Ibsen sense, of course, of that prurient phrase.

I enclose a snapshot in return: the view
from my Lower Broadway window. After dark
you can almost overlook the Hustler-Hut,

and the man in front of the all-graffiti wall
is none other than your ex. . . y. . . z. . . Can you tell
—the color's off—that I am smiling too?

2

Elizabeth dear, if slides are any clue
that place of yours is bliss! The garden path
down to the last primrose, must have been done

by Botticelli, or at least Burne-Jones. . .
I wish somebody would lead me up *that*.
Instead—of course you've heard, but just in case—

G has decamped—*for good*, as he says in the note
(so like him, isn't it? that righteous touch),
abandoning these puppies—I guess they're yours.

Anyway, do you want them? Do you want *him*, my dear?
When he came back, or to be frank came here
(I don't believe he saw it as a return,

more like a jumping-off place, a launching-pad)
I assume you found the riddance good. It seems
we are not punished for but *by* our sins,

so it is hard to be done with a man like G
once we've given him too much—of anything.
To tell the truth, you and I have been beguiled

by a phallus ex machina. . . Forgive me, dear, he does
bring out the bitch (which may not have been far in)
—he never kisses, and he always tells. . .

Such constant infidelity (do all roads lead
to Sodom?) certainly suggests that if one walks
so often through the grass (your lawn or mine)

one's likely to leave a path on which the sun,
if too many cocks crow, may not ever rise.
Here endeth the first lesson. Who needs more?

I'll be glad to drive the puppies to your place,
if you like. It occurs to me we might conduct
an original conversation. . . Now that I have

no one much to care for (and to care for me)
I fester, as you have perhaps perceived,
with unused (unusable?) human sympathy. . .

After all, I wanted just one thing in the world,
and that I may not have. So I am free
from what is called coveting. Of course we had

a number of tastes in common, G and I,
which for people with tastes at all can be a bond.
But who can halve his cake and serve it too?

I've got no education to speak of, but I have
a natural gift for window-dressing. All in all,
our talents pooled, we might have a splendid day,

and moreover, if neither one of us can lay
(whatever that means) poor G, perhaps we can,
by a kind of collusive confidence, lay his ghost.

3

Of course you must stay with us—come any time!
You wouldn't recognize the dogs (nor they you)
and who knows what "stay" means in your patois?

But nothing else has changed, the cedars soar
high over wave after wave of daffodils,
and the red admirals still do their saraband. . .

I always like to see a sailor dance.
As for Elizabeth—you must judge for yourself;
I'd say she must have felt, when you took off,

almost obsolete—just fancy, a widow
after seven months, and a clever woman too!
But where there is alcohol there is always hope.

Myself? I find little actually *changed*,
though flesh has become the word, so to speak.
I've never been so happy: nothing like sleep

to give yourself an appetite—who needs
the fugitive distress of lovemaking for that?
Some of me is stronger, some of me dead,

I've learned a little and forgotten more—
In sum, I am the same, dear, not so good
at making love as friendship; why, just now,

in the shower, you know, I took a serious look
and realized I resemble a Flaxman print:
the life-giver shrunk to an intercrural pimple. . .

There are three beehives in the orchard, remember?
I so enjoy watching the frightful little things:
oughtn't they to set me a classic example?

Or I them? Perhaps once you are here,
I'll get some honey and sit in front of the hives,
eating it leisurely (that much I've learned to do)

just to show them how life is to be enjoyed.
As you recall, Liz has an income of some size,
and *I* have that rarest gift, a genius for

reception. Certainly you will be bored,
but isn't that the whole point: *ennui à trois*,
emotion anticipated in tranquillity?

It might be regarded as chancy, given "our" pasts,
to have you here—between us, as it were.
But I doubt it. After all, someone must yield

to temptation or the whole thing turns absurd.
I long to see you and Lizzie arm in arm
or otherwise linked together. To be happy in 3's

is the proof of a talent for being happy at all.
I'll lace our first drinks with a little benzedrine,
I find that always makes a party go.

Famed Dancer Dies of
Phosphorus Poisoning

*said to be the consequence of many
years' exposure to costume
paint.* LE FIGARO, 1928

April 20, 1905

Dear Professor— No, my dear Madame,
English is my language, so I write
in that, although I am no writer at all
but a sort of daytime insomniac whose ink
has American notions of its own—but since
you have visited my country, I must hope
you make me out. . . I write to *you*, Madame,

rather than to your husband (though you both
might be addressed as Dear Professor, no?)
for you and I, in Paris, I perceive
are equally outsiders, and I trust
this may, between us, prove a bond.
We foreigners learn a busy lesson here:
the cure for loneliness is solitude.
Perhaps because the two of us are each

inside a place which by no accident
is known to the world as the City of Light,
my plea will strike you as appropriate
(a little like my dancing: something alive
and flexible, not going on too long).
The silver card you find enclosed admits
you and your party, any night you like,
to my box at the Folies-Bergère. You may have heard

of my endeavors on the stage: the Dance
of Wings, of Wands, the Meteor of Fear,
the Flame, the Lily, and the Butterfly. . .
But I am sure that if I were to bring
my efforts to your own inquiring gaze,
the chances of convincing you would be
far beyond what my uncertain words
might win—indeed beyond the wingèd ones

of Monsieur Anatole France himself, or those
of a greater master still, by some accounts,
Monsieur Auguste Rodin, who is my friend
and good enough to speak on my behalf:
I add their letters to my own appeal,
though I believe that what you see, yourself,
will work upon you more than *any* words,
even theirs. Let me persuade you by

all the liberal magic I have learned
to wield—another mode of creating life,
the poetry of an incarnate Now—
in order that *you* may capacitate my art
to cast a deeper spell. For once *you* see,
I know you will help me to be better seen. . .
My dancers have to move against a light
which cannot move: its source is fixed—

yet what if light itself could move—could dance?
The very darkness would be visible!
As I understand it, you have found the way
our costumes and our limbs themselves might be
made luminous, without depending on
the placement of a lamp or two offstage. . .
Endued with the substance which I hear you have named
by a happy inspiration *radium*,

we'd have no further need of phosphorus
which blackens in no time on human skin.
They say your new-found, final element
generates a light within itself
and would inspire—were you to let me have
the merest feather-touch of such a thing—
a freedom unsuspected by the world
of illusion which we artists live within.

I do not ask for charity, Madame—
only your presence, which I know would make
the soul of kindness the body of kindness too.
Come see my dancers, come see me! and if
you judge my craving worthy of my craft,
I know you will be generous. . . My warm
respects to your husband, and to you my hopes,
L. Fuller, or as they call me here, L A L O I E

Love Which Alters

for James Merrill

During the summer months of 1912
Reynaldo had been reading "our romance,"
for so he came to reckon it (at first
you love no longer, then long afterwards
you manage not to love), in paragraphs
and pages as it would be parcelled out:

fansticks, each fantastically carved
yet each a thing apart. . . For the life of him
he could not see how all of it would come
together, how each scene was set to shift
the next until the whole thing folded up,
collapsed by one mauve thread all through. . .

"You cannot see it for the life of you—
it won't be yours. *I* see it now, I know
the way it goes, the way it comes to me:
the freedom of the rosebush is the rose."
So much for authorship! Reynaldo read
what he was given, mystified, intent,

until on All Saints' Day—November first—
he was summoned. Clearly something had occurred.
"Bunchibils, I need your help—your ear,
just yours—you know what Madeleine is like
in arguments: as if you were dreaming the dream
where you appear in public quite undressed!

And Emmanuel is worse: he knows so much,
and what he knows is so abstruse, he finds
an answer absolutely out of the question
in terms of mere talk. Bunchibils, I need—
I need your bedside manner of the mind.
One word, Reynaldo: *what shall I call my book?*

It has become a book this time, I think,
and any number of names have come to light,
each replacing the next. Help me choose one.
How does it sound—*Stalactites of the Past?*
. . .*of Melted Days?* Is there a music in it—
Stalactites of Melted Days? Or how about

Reflections, wait, *Images—What is Seen
in the Patina. . . Mirrors of the Dream?
Belated Days?* Oh, I have others. Listen:
A Traveller in the Past—it must have that
at work inside it somewhere: I have nailed
my colors to *The Past.* What do you think

of this: *The Past Prorogued?* Oh yes you do—
when a case has been suspended or postponed
the court is said to be *prorogued.* You hear
the root of questioning in it, I like that:
interrogate—prorogue—I don't see why
people can't look things up, I always do.

All right then, what do you make of *The Past
Delayed. . . The Past Belated. . . The Past Erased?
A Visit to the Past?* Myself, I keep
coming back to *Reflections. . . Dreaming Glass*,
on the order of 'looking glass'. . . And still
The Days' Stalactite haunts me—Bunchibils,

43

are you listening? Of course I care,
it makes a difference, even if it is
only a tempest in my chamberpot,
as you so elegantly say. It matters to me
what stalactites are, and if they drip
down to their form or build up from the floor:

there must be something to intimate a pursuit
of the past: a visitor, a traveller. . .
I give you one week to winnow out a name.
Make it something like. . . like Christianity—
Good News, not good advice! Until you come
up with something, I shall be down with it,

with palpitations (if you know what they are).
This incapacity I feel to own
or to own up to memories is more
like a disease. Mine elude me still;
I cannot really make them mine except
at rare moments, in odd flashes. Perhaps

your method, Bunchibils, of taking them
to bed with you, is best. Perhaps what I want
I have already, here in what you've read.
Fine things are all the finer for being—a while—
forgotten. We shall brood, the two of us,
and breathe, Bunchibils! We need to breathe. . ."

Then on November seventh, as if there were
no doubt, no hesitation—as if in fact
alternatives had never been proposed,
the title appeared in a letter to Grasset:
"I want the whole experiment to be called
In Search of Lost Time. What you will bring out

next year is only an investiture, the roof
of the cave in which my deposits form themselves,
crystal by crystal. I enclose the proofs,
but only for the first two hundred sheets,
I need the rest to work on still—there are,
you will see, all sorts of changes to be made."

A Sorcerer's Apprentice

. . .And in your absence, Maestro, came to pass
the very visitation you foresaw
and fled. I would have done the same. Back home
in Italy, we even give a name
to such evasions: *going to Capri,*
we say, and make our getaway until
the danger passes. Danger always does.
So, there you were—in Capri. And he came
                    across the courtyard

as if he owned or soon would buy us all,
your caller—Caledonian by kilt
(even in Paris, to wear such a thing!),
Baedeker bulging from his Inverness,
Horace actually in hand, and kept
consulting, like a priest his missal, both—
prowled around the marble-stool where I
was busy sharpening the finer points
                    of his commission. . .

He watched me shift the calipers from clay
to stone to clay, and then began striding
up and down, as if to demonstrate
he had no patience for such enterprise;
grumbling followed, and more dramatic sighs
to signify the outrage of the case,
and for—or against—your return, left this
(devil's work for hands that have not learned
                    how to be idle):

Monsieur Rodin, I do not understand.
All was to be ready. So I read
the terms of the agreement you and I
drew up. I have it here. You recollect
how after looking through my cabinet
at Lewes House—a scholar's curios—
you made an offer I interpreted
as merely sociable (perhaps my chef
                 had surpassed himself):

"I am in love," you said, "with your *Ondine*.
I dream of having her—would you regard
the notion of an exchange as insolent?
If not, kindly say what piece of mine
might please you, marble or bronze, among the work
you praised when you came to Meudon last July—
perhaps we can reach an understanding." Then,
when I of course ignored such extravagance,
                 came wilder offers:

"I am disposed to trade my figure called
Walking Man (with legs apart) in wax
as well as the marble *Danaïd*—might this
pair, or some other, tempt you to part with your Nymph?"
And when I proved obdurate, you wrote yet again:
"Suppose I keep your *Ondine* only so long
as I live, and on my death she returns to you?"
Now I distinctly recall, Monsieur Rodin—
                 and what Scots recall

we recall distinctly—you *did* accept
my final terms (more formally expressed)
stipulating (1) that you yourself
select the marble, and retain *Ondine*
while, for a thousand pounds, within a year,
(2) you will devise a copy of the group
known today as *The Kiss*, but hitherto called
Paolo & Francesca, fashioned so
                the *membrum virile*

be molded, in this version, with the same
verisimilitude as any other part
of the lovers' flesh. I recapitulate
in such detail, Monsieur Rodin, because
you give me leisure to do so! Nor should I
have made a Channel crossing, were it not
for absolute assurances you made
to me yourself, acknowledging you had
                in the first instance

begged the question, showing what should be
proudly erect as no more than a prudent glow
in the stone, and that you would be glad
of the chance to do one properly. One what?
Where is the vaunted image to belie
Goethe's claim that only two things are
ugly: a penis and a crucifix?
I find you gone, and only your *praticien*
                toying with the task

for which you have received my thousand pounds
and the enjoyment, these eleven months
of my *Ondine*, delivered as duly pledged.
Your man was civil enough—indeed appeared
no ordinary labourer, and in command
of English to a degree—nevertheless
a garrulous artisan is no surrogate
for the hand of Auguste Rodin, and for the work
         which was our bargain.

Perhaps there is a reason for the lapse,
something so simple that even your workman
could not be invested with it—yet
if this were so, would he have prattled on?
I await some explanation at my hotel—
for the discourtesy, not for my chagrin
which needs no elaboration, and I trust
some remedy to my dissatisfaction. Yours,
        A L E X A N D E R G O W .

Maestro, the sheet lay open to all eyes,
of course I read it. Nor will you charge me with
prying, once I properly report
my intercourse with Gow—or his with me:
if I am to be called a prattler, let it be
in the service of what actually occurred,
and what did not. "My intercourse with Gow,"
I called it that myself. As soon as he saw
        how nearly complete

his sculpture was—how little, and how much,
remained to fulfill his covenant—he began
questioning: how you went about your work,
was there a model, who might that model be,
and—without a breath between—was the model I?
There is a kind of nosiness no one can
hold out against: with becoming modesty
I confessed myself the original for
                         Paolo's *cazzo*.

But did that suffice? No. Might not he,
to beguile the languors of the interval
till the Maestro returned—might not he
(he, Gow, begetter, as he claimed,
of this revision, being quite aware
that for all the Eternal Tunnels you have thumbed,
where was the Lifegiver's Tower? Surely not
the lumps in Balzac's bathrobe! Where indeed?
                         Why else was he here?)

Then might not he examine the *rapport*
between man's life and the art which it inspired?
Being the man in question, I begged off:
unless I held a false Francesca nude
here in my arms, the subject he desired
to scrutinize at closer range would be
unlikely to come up—if I said so
myself—to the fondest expectations of
                         either life or art.

Enough was said. Leaving this note behind,
Gow flung his cape around him and was off,
deceived by both of us, no doubt—though you,
Maestro, will make good—for a thousand pounds
and a borrowed *Ondine*—on a Scotchman's hopes,
with the index of a member mounting still
through incandescent marble: no longer dim
copulas of *The Kiss*, but distinct and huge. . .
                    Maestro, welcome home!

...*Always With You*

Canicule, and the first word you have had
from me since Spring—a shameful interval
wherein I parch with the piteous fields and wait

for rain, as they do. My dear Sir George,
alas I was not born with a pen in my mouth,
or in my hands, or toes! You may excuse

my silence the sooner, when you must compare
with it the solecisms of my speech:
I have grown rusty, rusticating here,

where a bird, if it be a bird in the hand, is dead,
and death is Nature's principal salute. . .
I wish—I *begin* to wish—to be in Town:

willow-trees, waterfalls and wasteland, while
choice occasional cronies, take their toll
by constant companionship. I feel I fail,

confederated so, and lose my bravery—
August has drained me of *courage*, in the sense
the word achieves when Chaucer lays it to

the energy of primaveral larks.
I write you now from that Moss-Hut of mine
which serves for cabinet, the sun meanwhile

tyrannical round about; this is a place
of retirement for the eye, though a Public Road
glimmers through the apple-trees beneath,

and soberly coupled with my labours—yet
I cannot keep from smiling, drought and all,
at the scenes I am made to witness here betimes.

Item, the other morning, when I sat
calling some lofty notes out of my harp,
chaunting of Shepherds and Solitude, etc.

I heard a voice, which I reckoned to be male,
crying out from the road below, in a tone
exquisitely effeminate: "Fetch it here,

fetch, Pandore, come come come come COME!"
Now who might the vagrant be, to volley so
with his lap-dog amid our venerable peaks?

One of a pair of popinjays who have hired
for the long vacation the Cottage we had hoped
might suit you, and who *will* parade themselves

about our Valley in garb of every kind—
fantastic garments, green-leather capes,
Turkey half-boots, tiny jackets of lawn

or long dressing-gowns, as please them best.
Now we hear one (singing!) in the dale,
and now espy one lolling in such attire

as might engage a Favorite of King James
to wonder if this jerkin and that hat
might with these trousers run to Motley—all

to furnish, in the year 1806,
appropriate apparel for the hour,
the day, the season, and the circumstance:

a book (what book it might be, God forbid
the knowledge thereof! but an undoubted book)
in hand by a brook-side. Frequently they pass

our window in their curricle, horses one day
in tandem and the next abreast, then saddled
as flatters their fancy. One of them we suspect

is painted, yet the other—as chalk to cheese—
not to be outdone by his blooming sib,
affects a pigmentation that would shame

pale Hamlet's cast of thought. One may indulge
such creatures for their very *bizarrerie*!
If you came out, you should see them for yourself,

and perhaps believe; yet I had rather far
see *you* in London. Till that time may be,
I have procured for the pinnace a set of sails

and tomorrow shall give my fortunes to the wind
if a wind on Derwentwater may be raised
in these Dog-Days (and though our dog appear

no better than "Pandore": a creature half
demon-bat and half demented kit—
proper *immoment toy* of such a pair).

The clouds forbear to darken counsel—may
the spell dissolve! My head is filled with stars
not yet arrayed—our Wilderness forbids—

into constellations. Behold, then, how I am
entertained, and by what Company!
Faithfully, WM WORDSWORTH. *At Rydall Mount.*

The Foreigner Remembered
by a Local Man

Fuseli! I fancied the floor would tumble down—
could he be less than a giant, genius itself?
Footsteps approached, then a bony little hand

slid round the doorframe, followed presently
by a lion-faced, white-haired pygmy of a man
in a gown of old flannel gathered round his waist

by a length of rope, and wearing on his head
what I made out with some surprise to be
the bottom of Mrs Fuseli's sewing-basket. . .

My work was there. The Maestro stared about.
"By Godde," said he, "you will nefer paint finer.
It vas alvays in you, I haff said, and now,

by Godde, it is out! You have de touch—it is
Wenetian entirely. But you look demn tin!"
To such a point our converse fired him up

we drove instanter to Park Lane, the while
he swore like a fury—a very little one—
yet how relentless was his vehemence

as he strode among the marbles, filled with zeal:
"De Greeks vere Goddes, Goddes vere dey." It proved
a scene immortal in my sanguine life. . .

So far from London's smoke offending me,
it has always seemed sublime, a canopy
shrouding the City of the World. "By Godde,"

Fuseli said as we took the air that day,
"it is de smoke of Israelites making bricks."
"Grander, sir," said I: "it is the smoke

of a people who in freedom would have forced
the Egyptians rather to make bricks for them."
"Vell done, John Bull!" Fuseli cried aloud.

And now, this morning, Reynolds came: "He's gone."
"Who, sir?" "Fuseli." "A man of Genius. . ." "But
I fear of no principle." "Why, sir, say you so?"

"He has left, I hear, such drawings—quantities
shockingly indelicate." I had no heart
to finish my figure. Today must be a blank. . . .

Mademoiselle's Last Sunday

Not the wages. How could I have faced
so long your own indifference and Madame's
—of hers I do not trust myself to speak—
for nothing more than money? No, Monsieur,

I had not remained within—you call it so?—
the Bosom of your Family to this day
were it not for Cameron. Your son requires
I shall not say *myself*, but someone there

to answer for a world you do not choose
to share. That is my cause—why I am here.
Surely he has said enough for you to know
as much? We learn not French together but

perhaps a little love, a little reason. So
when I fail—as I have failed today—
my only test for being here, I go. . .
Of course I have told him! Cameron at six

will understand my going better than
anyone in this house. Please to assume
as much responsibility as a child
—I do not ask for references even—

and listen to what occurred. Hear me out
—he's perfectly all right, he's in his room;
no harm has come to him: he was with me,
but I can no longer be accountable. . .

We were waiting for the métro, at Oberkampf,
after our visit to the Wax Museum
(Bluebeard, Landru, all the reprobates
were reproduced), and in the little crowd

along the platform was this. . . individual
—I know he was drunk, perhaps diseased as well—
who seemed to find us offensive: Cameron
and me! our clothes? our closeness? or perhaps

too many questions in a child's high voice?
No one seemed to mind that a *clochard* went on
screaming abuse at the two of us. It was
an ugly moment, I knew we must get away,

when across the tracks, on the Porte de Lilas *quai*,
a man of my own age, quite well-dressed,
opened his attaché-case and removed,
carefully closing the clasps, snap snap,

what I think was a machete—I know it was.
And then with great deliberation (while
the screaming continued: Cameron and I
still paralyzed) he climbed down to the rails,

stepping over each one to the other side,
our side, and up onto the platform where
quite calmly, with one sharp thrust to the neck
he killed—I knew it at once—our unknown foe

and walked—Monsieur, he walked away! No more
than when that lunatic was shouting filth,
now that he lay bleeding at our feet
was there a movement: no one in that crowd

moved, Monsieur! Cameron kept asking me
all the way home—we took a taxicab—
why that man was shouting at us, why
that other man had come across the tracks

to kill him with his. . . weapon as if he knew
the thing would be of use, as if. . . as if. . .
I had no answer then, I have none now,
Monsieur. I do not know. And I must leave

Cameron and my place—oh, not because
I cannot explain why such a thing occurred
—all of us are ignorant, Monsieur—
nor even because of the *joy* I had in that death

—why should I forsake the child for that:
desertion would be a self-indulgence, no?
It is not for my ignorance or joy. It is
because of Cameron's elated questioning:

"Can we play métro as soon as we get home?"
and because I know what playing means, Monsieur,
and you do not. You *shall*! Nor do I care
that Cameron must live forever seeing it.

So must I. We all want truth on our side,
but to be on the side of truth—do we want that?
Cameron is in his room, playing. Alone.
I have said what is necessary to your son,

perhaps you will make my excuses to Madame.
I leave you with no notion what I shall do,
though certain I shall not seek another place.
No teaching. No telling. No knowing. *Au revoir.*

Concerning K

Not one breath. Even the flags had. . .flagged.
Decades of usurpation and fatigue
foreground these polaroids—the postcards lie—
and every street in Prague appears to lead
to a blackened sepulchre. Nowhere to go,

unless one is in the Market for Fleas. Why not?
The Festival was over, they had crowned
and drowned in Tokay poetry's Clown Prince,
Don Giovanni had (again) been foiled,
and the charter flight was bumped another day.

Mitteleuropa was up for sale, piecemeal;
picking desultorily through the booths,
you and the person we both call X fell out:
"—infinitely desirable—" "—Bohemian dreck—"
over the daub you photographed "for me". . .

Boredom, according to Walter Benjamin,
is a brood-hen on the egg of experience:
a rustle in the leaves will drive her off.
Not one sound. Tenantless the leaves
hung from every willow, every oak.

At least those booths were cooler than the street.
So that was where you found it, in the dark
(as what was not, in the rabid city—gnostic,
rabbinical, patristic, kabbalistic): *dark*
was the distempering of discovery!

Painted in darkness, out of darkness too,
and dubiously meant, on muddy duck,
for a martyred Saint manacled to a stump,
the carcass oddly cavernous for being
so gaunt, more oddly luminous for being

so terribly hard to make out. . . But you did
—if not with X—make out (forgive me!) Saint
Sebastian. . . Who else? What other throes could be
so eagerly submissive, so thrilling, so lewd?
And the model! Could anyone else have stood

even a moment for what your letter calls
"a morbid appetite for arrows"? The moral is:
Don't pose as a Saint or you may become one. . .
Not one of the Happy Many, who suffer so far
and then collapse, exhausted, over and out;

just the opposite—the more a Saint suffers,
the fiercer the energy summoned to endure.
This Saint, or the human violence that masks
his sanctity in martyrdom's masquerade,
is beyond mere pain. He needs no doctrine,

only opportunities. Here is a good one:
the soul unties its shoes, pulls off its socks,
and stands revealed. Still life is still life,
and ears apart—apart from what? Part bat!—
the body you identified (and *coveted*?)

is geometrically impossible, the parts
greater than the whole. Which you wanted to buy?
Own? Haul back to. . .me, I guess. For once,
X and reason prevailed. Imagine possession—
forever to face such darkness, and such light!

The self, divine in each of us, is not
to be fully entered into. Manifest here,
or there, whereof these polaroids report
enough. I know about as much of Prague
as he—your precious, phantasmatic Saint—

knew of Amerika. Photographs transform
space into time, any image will do,
and does: leathery oils whose lesson is clear
(disdain for the world is not love of God)
and whose identity is plain as day:

Kafka writes in his diary for 1912
The painter Ascher has asked me to pose
for a Saint Sebastian. I am to pose nude.
Let it rot in Prague where you found the thing.
X spots the mark. You must resume your life.

Stanzas in Bloomsbury

*(Mrs Woolf entertains the notion
of a novel about Lord Byron)*

> *. . .wanting to build up my
> imaginary figure with every
> scrap I could find, when
> suddenly the figure turns to
> merely one of the usual dead. . .*

In search of treasure near the Pyramids
they all become unconscionably coy
having unearthed a vessel tightly sealed
secluded special and being set upon
opening it they found that it contained
one object which they all agreed to be
honey by taste till hairs clinging to
just what was wanted—though it seemed to me
the private parts of an intrepid man
merely silly and tinkling as if once
drawn forth what met their eyes was a boy
—I had ventured into the men's urinal!
his limbs entire the flesh smooth what else
but lust and tenderness afford relief?

Each man is under his thumb—just conceive
living your life in fear of drying up
and on command plunging from the walls
though haven't envisaged that fate for myself
enticed with hope of inevitable paradise—
on the contrary shall I ever have time enough
and promise of pleasure—eternal ecstasy
to write out everything that's in my head

ordering this one or that to leap to his doom
—though suppose what's in my head becomes absurd
for the entertainment of others, after which
—but would I even know it afterwards?
still others were pledged that night for their desires
besides I cannot believe I shall ever die. . .

I thank you for the bishop's work on God
which I am reading though he prove no more
than what I have always thought: so I am
not impotent but I have had enough
where I was—verging toward Spinoza not
of a mind to write books but to become
alien to his gloomy creed—I would be
nice to other people (only now? this once?)
better than that? there is a power in me
obsessed beyond all reading to withstand:
I cannot shake it off. I deny nothing
of all the accumulation of the past
but doubt everything. Incessant guests
are quite as bad as solitary jail.

Colored Stones

for Robin Utterback

(A T H E N S)

Marble, said the guide, a marble mount!
Step by step the Acropolitan
ascent rehearsed—disclosed—our Pilgrimage,
Americans, more Germans, even Greeks.
The Way was ready for us as we came:
whatever we were, the white stones would wear.

(H O U S T O N)

Fifty feet away, the buildings look
bullet-pocked, but closer to, each hole
turns out to be a scallop or a snail.
The walls are beaches then! a fossil shore
has taught the lessons of Old Main:
Thalassa! Thalassa! the Ten Thousand cried.

(A L B U F E I R A)

Those rusty-looking piles offshore? *Three Nymphs*
the locals call them, though *I* can make out
no more than a messy form of bricolage;
here on the wrong side of Gibraltar the sea
can oxidize a nymph into a nun
(Atlantic orders, iron-grey and dun).

Colored Stones

(W O O D S T O C K)

Bluestone quarries. This was where they cut
the sidewalks of New York, which do not seem
particularly blue. And giving way
to asphalt and macadam, gravel, dust.
Here the walls of fine-grained boulders glow;
sometimes, "in city pent," a fine blue must.

(S I R A C U S A)

Bristling with cannas, Dionysos's Ear
(a cave above the quarry where Greeks died)
shelters a deft ropemaker who demonstrates
for tourists daily. Sleek golden walls
set off his art, and only cannas share
the crimson shame of Alcibiades.

(W I S C A S S E T)

Braided black and white, the waves repeat
or imitate the rocks of Pemaquid;
these are the interferences of quartz
with granite, some archaic violence
garish as light on water. Stone to sand,
sea to sun, identical returns.

(T O U R S)

Companioned by the Loire whose limestone cliffs
punctuate a classical landscape, pale
as if they had seen the ghost of Italy,
we turned off, down a lane not on the map,
and before us spread a whited precipice,
the shining slate-capped castle of Chambord!

(B R Y C E   C A N Y O N)

A whirling snowstorm out of nowhere—so
we say, but into nowhere too is more
like it—and all the Utah boulders turned
from red that had the truth of massacre
to merely mass, no color and no truth:
the ruined rocks under the ruthless snow.

(C O Z U M E L)

"A stone in the road—it had to be a stone
to keep that still as the car bore down." "No,
the shock was not the indifferent adieu
of rock and rubber. Stop. See what it. . .was."
The pebbled hide lay open: lilac and pink,
entrails of an iguana still alive.

(C A M D E N)

"I find I incorporate gneiss and coal, stucco'd
all over," Whitman wrote, and I have been
to the low house (he drew it for himself)
where such incorporation still goes on.
The great stones make a tiny Stonehenge there,
and the poet becomes his good gray grave.

(III)

ORACLES

TO THE MEMORY OF
VERA LACHMANN
(1905–1985)

Not here. I must be out of the wind,
   under something—otherwise
I cannot light these insipid weeds
   alleged to be cigarettes.
Even they are forbidden, of course,
   but it is too late to mind
or at least, at my age, to matter . . .
   Yes, here: this will do. *In time,*
they say: *time heals*—though what can that mean
   to men your age? What have you
to heal? Myself, I cannot afford
   waiting much longer to heal,
always a matter of waiting, no?
   When it comes to *doing time*
here is the place: Greece knows how to wait.
   Meanwhile, as you young men say
(and mean well by it, though you will learn
   that no moment *replaces*),
I have made what my physician calls
   a massive recovery—
I suppose he is telling the truth:
   the only men you can ask
honesty from are the men you pay
   to get it from. I have paid . . .
Enough to let me smoke a little,
   if I really have recovered.
Not much of an exploit, once they set
   a machine inside your heart:
after all, what is the heart itself
   when you come to think of it
but a mortal machine? In my case
   somewhat less reliable

than most machines, somewhat more
mortal. In *any* case, though,
all a heart has is the *eminent*
dignity* of a machine,
like so many Swiss inventions—banks
and boredom and . . . chocolate.
And since that emplacement (I am spared
the details), my condition
—that is what I have, a *condition*—
is serious, but neither
fatal nor severe; it is merely
something that I remember
on certain occasions, like a poem
(what we say about ourselves
is always poetry). It would be
offering ignominy
to the gods, perhaps, to live happy
and well to the end: the gods
exist because men are ill, and as
Anatole France used to say,
the gods' impotence is infinite. . . .
Best to grow old like the rest
in a *mingled* manner, consonant
with an ordinary fate.
I have been happy and well this spring—
too happy, I fear, to be
really well. Understand me: I have
glorious days, and conclude
that a degree of physical pain
renders happiness perfect.
The best thing to be said for old age
—of course we do not always
or even often say the best thing—
is that it is the one means
discovered to this day for living
a long time.

. . . I should have thought
such intuitions wasted on you:
we never believe others'
experience, and only inchmeal
will you be won over by
your own. Think of all the boys who died
young as you—too young to have
learned their own wisdom. Though their own minds
were active as phosphorus,
they died in whispers they did not hear . . .
So I am taken aback
or perhaps it is forward—at least
I am stirred up, seeing
you fellows return so readily
for another dose of these
mischievous commonplaces of mine,
just when I had decided
that to be heard out as an old bore
is *the* ineluctable
consequence of one's declining years.
(Boredom too has its prestige—
which the reason knows nothing about.)
But then you are after—or
into, that is what you inquiring
Americans say nowadays—
you are into something specific?
Never mind the *properties*;
I shall tell you what I know, even if
today you find me looking
rather frail and untrustworthy in
a far too suggestive and
actually Japanese dressing gown . . .
Dislike of modernity
and of outdatedness are in fact
identical; hence my . . . garb.
Of course it is a disguise; there is

little likelihood of "truth"
    whenever feelings of pleasure have
        any say in the matter.
Proof of pleasure is pleasure itself—
    nothing more. I cannot take
my time gracefully, but I take it:
    flesh was never intended,
as Nikisch once said of *Pelléas*,
    to be a success. The most
I can hope for is to age like wine,
    not ferment like vinegar.
You follow me? You are back again,
    so I suppose you must. . . .
Ours is a comfortable doom, here:
    just as someone said *un ours*
et c'est la paix, so it is with me:
    un mécanisme et la santé
s'est retrouvée. Or very nearly.
    (You understand what I have said?
French is spoken in every language,
    even on this old island
where the dialect sounds like water
    draining out of a bathtub!).

Very well then, however ill: here
    I lay, tastefully buried
in my texts—my pretexts—quite content
    to be dusted off only
during seizures of necrophilia,
    dozing till you dug me out
—excavated me, that is the word—
    from this classical soil,
all too honorifically lodged
    in this Harmless Institute
for Hopeless Scholars, groggy by night
    and gaga by day. You know

my colleagues? You have looked us over,
  examined the . . . specimens?
Except for myself—whom I regard
  as a *foregone conclusion*—
there is in some sense no single woman
  on this island—only wives.
Quite possibly they were women once
  and have deteriorated. . . .
I dine with them sometimes—to improve
  the moral tone—theirs or mine,
Who knows? They have done up each "guest room"
  in the place to resemble
the cell of a rather pansy monk—
  Marimekko drapery
and *tofu*—no, *futon* on the floor . . .
  Modern man wants to sleep close
to the ground, like animals: we
  furnish ourselves with matting,
do away with the bed, and thereby
  annul the human threshold
between waking and dreaming. We dream,
  of course, on our sleek pallets
—even scholars-in-retirement dream—
  but who knows how such décor,
queer as it is, affects us? Between
  "it came to me in a dream"
and "I dreamed" lie ages of the world,
  but which is truer: spirits-
who-send-dreams or an-ego-that-dreams?
  We are not awake because
we have done away with the dream, but
  only when we have swallowed
the dream once more, and digested it. . . .

  As for our Scholars themselves—
you know, Goethe says a celibate group

can create the greatest works,
but an old bachelor will seldom
produce anything sensible.
Equally true of old widowers.
    They would be glad to renounce
all Kant and Spinoza to possess
    the memoirs of Aspasia. . . .
Most of them have been rendered deaf by
    hearing the birds sing in Greek
(as they do, but not to the exclusion
    of all other languages):
deaf men, but alas quite the reverse
    of dumb; courteous though, and
of course they can be altogether
    engaging—with just a hint
of the usual halitosis—
    to outsiders.

                . . . No duties. None.
We *do* nothing here, month after month
    —it is nothing, to offer
one lecture each summer to young men
    like yourselves, you *listeners*!
Words are the opium of the West—
    syllables seduce the world,
and history does not merely touch
    language, it takes place *in it*;
the day will come when we each have turned
    into a dictionary:
the substance of things hoped for—our faith!
    Till then we give our lectures.
Even this year, mine went off quite well—
    just one pause when I forgot
what I was going to say next and
    suddenly heard my watch *tick*
tick tick until I realized: *that*

is my heart! A fine moment.
All the moments are fine now, all days
   simple. As if in a trance . . .
Perhaps it is not me but some other
   woman, one who likes passing
absurdity under your nostrils
   like a wine connoisseur
extolling old brandy—another
   woman in an unpossessed
place, the future of her memories,
   sitting by this silent sea.
When you believe *I am I* and *she*
   is she, you are unconscious;
when you believe *I am she* and *she*
   is I, you are cognizant. . . .
One more of my formulas.

                 Young man,
   I know what you are thinking;
you are thinking I must be a witch
   or at least a wise-woman,
something of a sibyl, but I warn you:
   be cautious here, lest shallow
call to shallow. This is modern Greece!
   Have you not learned what that means?
We are wide awake, and this island,
   once the place of prophecy,
is the site of a Scholars' Retreat
   which combines the infantile
and the degenerate—or perhaps
   it is merely innocence
and inevitability? No,
   you must not be fooled by such
dissimulations. My gown hangs round
   what is left of my body
like classical draperies . . . .

                        Hellas!
      To most people, classicism
means *work in class*, and as my mother
    who knew—knew intimately—
Professor Wilamowitz-Moellendorff
    used to say (though not to him):
an hour is enough of anything. . . .

      You see, we are all alike,
we Eminent Germans—not so much
    the pupils as the victims
of history. Perhaps that is why
    we write as we do: because
the expression of history in things
    is precisely that of past
torment. . . . We Germans are the people
    unable to tell a lie
without believing it ourselves. And
    by now you must have observed
our horror of adults with no degrees,
    or at least with no titles . . . .
Eminent Germans always seem to be
    swimming deep underwater—
only Nietzsche, that lonely dolphin,
    plays on the sparkling surface. . . .
Here, at least, we drown in Aegean
    radiance! Is that why you
—even you fellows—come here to lie
    on these beaches, these black stones,
like so many lizards in the sun?
    No wonder you take me for
some kind of Circe. . . .
                 As I explained,
    I have no magic powers.
I am something of a prisoner

myself, for all liberties
taken, for all licenses given:
   I cannot go up or down—
that is natural. I must abide
   by the level of things, not
venture very high (no danger there)
   or very deep . . . . But until
you have attained, or been attained by,
   my years, you cannot conceive
how much depends on mere surfaces. . . .
   Why "mere"? Say *sheer* surfaces,
steep as these Cycladic palisades—
   that is where the meanings hide.
In the gods' life, what we understand
   is the moment they lie *hid*:
if I tell you this place is holier
   than others, I only mean
more holiness has run out of it.
   Appearances are apparitions!
What would a god be without weaving
   appearances round himself,
or Aphrodite without a cloud
   to protect her? Imagine
a goddess *worse for wear*! Meanings hide
   in surfaces, that much I know.
Where else could they go?

               Truly, I have
   lied so much about my age
I forget how old I really am. . . .
   I think I look sixty-five,
I *admit* to eighty, and some days
   when the wrong wind manages
to make its way around the corner
   of the *taverna* terrace
I know I feel a hundred and ten!

We become, gradually,
as old as we look, and by the time
    we look and have the same age,
it will be all over. . . . I can wait.
    We are made out of nothing,
Valéry is right, but what we are
    made of keeps showing through . . . .

                                                    All

is nothing, but afterwards: after
    everything has been endured.
Till then, everything is something
    other than what it is. . . .
You are not likely to make much of
    what I have just said to you. . . .
But then, you are not likely
    to be here. . . . What is *likely*?
It is an irony, it is even
    a paradox you should be
asking for these reminiscences,
    these webs I have been spinning
so long—God forbid you might call them
    ideas! *Those* my colleagues have,
and from my colleagues I have learned: all
    fabrication of ideas
is evasion of a story . . . But
    for all my stories—have I
even told you one? Have I begun?
    —and my storytelling, too:
I am not like what I have professed
    in those learned articles
of mine, footnoted so flagrantly
    (the test of a vocation,
after all, is how much you can love
    the drudgery it involves).
I am a woman of learning, not

wisdom. I have been granted
the liberty of those who have ceased
to circulate, and it is
remarkable how . . . true to itself
   life becomes, how *transparent*,
once one is no longer part of it . . . .

No, *I am no oracle*,
though there are certain observations
   I have come to share, certain
intuitions you might call *mantic*
   (if you wished—like my colleague
counting up aorist variants
   in the closet next to mine—
to keep them from taking any part
   in your memory). For me,
the world is a living animal—
   not an immutable form,
but waxing and waning—not to be
   coerced or calculated,
but something unforeseen that we learn
   by initiation, not
by experiment, a vital force . . .
   The world is subject only
to choice, not to solution—it is
   a *figure*: one I observe—
if it matters what I do . . . .
                     I have
Gibbonian apprehensions:
it seems to me that an extinction
   of all art is prefigured
in our growing incapacity
   to represent history—
historical events. To us the past
   always appears as destroyed
by catastrophes. Perhaps it is,

        perhaps that is our tradition.
    Adequately to hate tradition
        one must have it in oneself. . . .

    For sure my fears are not Pythian:
        I have not suffered the one
    fate that really is "more dire than death"—
        beyond death, canceling death:
    the loss of my own identity . . . .
        No doubt you can tell—it is
    what I cannot bear to relinquish. . . .

    There you are, at last we come
—*finalmente mia*—to a chapter
    of the story, I should say
stories, theirs as well as mine, this time . . . .
    A little anthropology
is a dangerous thing: when *I* came
    to the end of the story
brought to light here—the shrine, the priestess,
    the responses of the god—
having followed the last residues
    of the law's millennium,
I gave up any claim I might have
    to *oracular wisdom*. . . .
Call it a failure of nerve—call it
    anything. What was *practiced*
on this island, and on others too,
    was not prophecy, it was
deliverance. That is what I learned:
    Sacred Games in which the lost
god was recovered, by a change from
    sorrow to joy, from darkness
and sights of inexplicable terror
    to light: the discovery
of a god reborn. You can see why

there were worshippers before
there were gods—the ritual always
    precedes the divinity. . . .
It is why the Oracle had been,
    so long, a woman: you are
a man, or become one, only by
    ceasing to be a woman. . . .
Even Jesus gave up his mother—
    he too was a man, of sorts. . . .
Till the third century, responses
    came out of a woman's mouth,
out of her body: answers given
    at once, without reflection
and without interruption. She was
    entheos: a god was in her.
And if she answered "wrong," that was
    because she answered at all—
real answers are not something outside
    the question. Age after age,
the world around these islands *believed*
    and was prepared to believe,
purifying, offering, waiting. . . .
    Have we any conception
of the demand on her? Of the weight?
    At Patara, she would be
chained inside the temple after dark
    so the god could get at her,
enter her—his medium, his lips . . . .
    (It was the first witticism
I ever made in English without
    translating: for the priestess
to be entered was to be entranced—
    entrance was entrancement . . .) So.
And when there was no more such speaking—
    when "oracle" was the same
patronizing disparagement as

"testicles," your tiny heads—
then the voices fell silent or turned
fickle, even menacing.
Pausanias tells of one Pythia
beguiled to attempt her trance,
even though the omens were adverse—
her words could not be made out:
hoarse noises, as if her throat was filled
by "recalcitrant spirits"—
screaming as she fled from the altar,
whereupon everyone fled,
even her attendants, and found her
apparently recovered,
yet within a few days she perished. . . .
It is a form of proof that
everything believed—and nothing else—
exists. You ask me about
a change—I see you have heard something
of Pythian *replacements*—
boys for virgins . . . All of it began,
perhaps, with that death. A sort
of admonition to try elsewhere . . . .
You know, I believe events
occur in series—nothing happens,
then several things happen
in quick succession, as though life
had been gathering up strength
over a long time for an effort. . . .
Unofficial oracles
—by rights a contradiction in terms—
were first heard of in such times:
esoteric cults, séances held
in sacred places, sometimes,
but hesitantly: what was the use
of a temple, people asked:
a temple is the place where men weep

together. Now there would be
    no weeping, but pleasure and the god's voice—
        the god's voice would be pleasure.
An oracle was consulted "at home,"
        by citizens at their ease,
and among these there would be a man
        known as the *pelistikê*
who tried to incarnate the god's voice
        in *katochoi*, mediums . . . .
This done by fair means or foul—*fair* meant
        smearing the eyes with nightshade,
and *foul* meant sexual possession.
    The modes tended to become
identical: whether you immersed
        your *katochos*—largely yours,
by now, because you had paid the price—
        in brimstone and sea-water,
or joined the jabbering creature in
        a parodic communion,
your fingers driven about the flesh
        with such heat that in your haste
to have the divine message, they seemed
        to smoulder and burst into flame—
ceased to make much of a difference . . . .
    The most suitable of such
partners were supposed to be persons
        "young and simple"—mainly boys:
Minucius Felix jeers and calls them
        Prophets without a Temple,
vates absquet templo . . . I have found
        recipes for casting them
into the proper trance state—it seems
        to have been *de rigueur*
to invite the god by erotic
        excitement. Reluctantly
at first, the god came more readily

once the habit had been formed
of entering the same vessel. . . . We know
of one boy, Aesidius,
who had only to stare intently
into scented coals: at once
he fell into a trance, as well as
your arms, and out of him came—
as he stirred, witlessly murmuring
under your touch, oracles,
reliable ones, in the highest
inspirational manner.
Of course you heard in the words he spoke
only what was already
in you, but to know what was in you
you needed the words spoken,
and for this the motions of "passion"
were indispensable. So
you could regard these boys as trophies
of action, as instruments
of knowledge. That was not their function.
Their function was to revolt
—being adolescents—against themselves
and thus to release a god.
The cues of induction could be learned—
anything at all distinct
from daily life, whatever was odd
would suffice: bathing in smoke
or dressing in "magical" chitons.
Moreover, as you may guess,
manifest profits were to be made—
although provisionally:
it appears that when these children grew
accustomed to such methods,
when they came to *enjoy* the treatment
received at their masters' . . . hands—
they no longer resisted the pneuma

sufficiently to obtain
worthwhile responses. If there was
no pain, no tension, there was
no sacred word. You cannot step twice
    —if I may put it this way—
into the same stream of consciousness. . . .

Such matters should be left to
women: we are so much more equal
    to them than men. Consider,
for instance, the female animal,
    her fear of copulation:
to her it must bring nothing but pain:
    merely listen to the cats—
pleasure is a late acquisition.
    When you watch the animals
spellbound in their intercourse, you see
    how the females undergo
love in bondage, objects of violence. . . .
    Women know this still, even
now, and a memory of the old
    injury persists.
                    Of course
I learned more than I . . . I learned too much:
    the special knowledge I gained—
what in religion is often called,
    by the blind, revelation—
has defeated me. I cannot bear
    to remember what I know.
And perhaps I am wrong, knowing it:
    perhaps the boys were . . . useful,
after all. Does pleasure presuppose
    in those whom it has chosen
a limitless readiness to throw
    oneself away? It is past
women in their wisdom—it is past

grown men in their arrogance.
You must be very religious indeed
   to change your religion. . . .
These women who served the shrine for life,
   who bathed and drank from sacred
vessels and by chewing the laurel
   held intercourse with the god—
even those boys, not that much younger
   than yourselves, I imagine,
whored out to the offhand appetites
   of the spiritually dim,
seem to have learned what I . . . .
                     No,
   not what I have lost sight of:
I am not blind. Nor did I fail to
   learn. I learned. I did not fail
to understand, and understanding
   has not failed me. I simply
—simply!—did not *practice* what I learned.
   I just learned . . . .
            Without the world's
assistance we cannot see two things:
   our face and our life in time.
To know the first, we must have mirrors;
   to see the second, clocks.
Once possessed of these, we inhabit
   a world bereft of the gods.
Can you understand me? It is why
   I have abandoned pursuit
of what I once so merrily, once
   so mercilessly studied.
Gentlemen, I am opaque; I know
   everything I must do, while
those boys, for example, had only
   to let themselves be devoured.
I am not worthy. . . . And my colleagues,

controverting each other
into fame, are not worthy of me!
    Listen to them: an abstract
and purely individual tact
    becomes no more than . . . lying:
how we dupe each other over meals,
    where silence is the rule, since
taboos on talking shop and distaste
    for talking to each other
are in reality the same thing. . . .

So you find me here, alone,
one of those intellectuals who are
    the last foe of the bourgeois
and the last bourgeois—an exile from
    my own world and an alien
in theirs . . . waiting for the flood! Ever
    since we were said to "rise,"
we bourgeois have waited for the flood. . . .
    Now here you are, and although
you are not quite what I call the flood,
    I am glad you flushed me out,
enchanted you returned for a new . . . spell.
    It is wonderful to live
with spirits of the great—with the dead—
    but one must meet the living
to secure a sense of one's own worth. Nor
    would I give the impression
of asceticism—that is an aspect
    I am eager to avoid,
being under the strictest orders
    from that physician of mine
to laugh at least twice a week. I wish
    my dentist were more of a help. . . .
But you are not to think of me as
    a tragic figure, should you

think of me at all. I shall remain
  here until all the voices
cease, and dust has filled the path of Greece. . . .
    What . . . extrication it is,
living without anticipating,
    dying quite regularly:
I sometimes think I should like to have
    the rest of my insides out
—taken right out—and machines put in
    for the lot. It would be best
not to know what such things as the lungs,
    the spleen and the gall-bladder
might be, if one were willing to press
    a human creature against
oneself with any fervor at all. . . .
    You, I suppose, are willing,
are you not? And you will marry, too—
    young men marry, even if
they are obliged to discover wives
    at the top of a bookcase. . . .
Men appear to find their wives
    in strange places . . . Adam
found his in himself; many find theirs
    in other people's beds, and
my father's friend, Professor Mommsen,
    found his in his cook!
                No,
I see . . . It is not marrying, but
    burning that is your fate. So.
And that is why you asked . . . Why you came
    here, and why you came to me!
I have no heart, as I told you, but
    my brains are in the right place:
my mind works best when it is almost
    too late. I shall tell you, then,
how it was with the boy. . . .

On the night
you decide on Aesidius,
you will be taken without warning
in the dark, bathed, anointed
by other holy boys, you will drink
water brought from Lethe's spring,
and you will forget who you are. Then
you will study a secret
image and be robed in white linen
bound with the sacred fillets—
only then, the omens favoring,
will you be conducted down
the ladder into a dark place where
the boy Aesidius will
receive from you—his body from yours—
the divine message, swiftly
articulated. Merely put your
hand under his arm: the god
that is in him will pass between you
though of course this cannot be
comprehended by either of you. . . .
The consequence of certain
anomalies is to emphasize
what is normal: so you may
learn if what we have called normal is
reality . . . or torpor.
Your pleasure may leave *you*, but he will
keep it, solidify it,
enrich it: he will transform the time
of a minor occasion
which you have managed to share into
realizations whereby
you will be enlightened, as temples
are gilded: and who can say—
perhaps such anointing will endure. . . .
Then you will drink

from Mnemosyne's spring, in order
to remember afterward
what has been revealed. . . .

                        What has been . . . I
have said enough. You should be
leaving before I tell everything—
    Moses, you know, probably
said to himself: *must stop before I*
    tell everything, that is why
there are only Ten Commandments.
                             No,
    I can get back by myself
perfectly well. Thank you for coming—
    I shall not, in leave-taking,
tell you, as English-speaking people
    often tell *me*, to "relax,"
to "take it easy." Such formulas
    are borrowed from the language
of the nursing home, not from active
    life. Just . . . *wiedersehen*. Our talk
has enlivened me a little, even
    talk of my own derision
and discouragement: knowing one has
    no body left to speak of,
one cannot entertain the god, *ripe*
    for the tripod, so to speak,
not when one is shriveled to seed. No
    restraint is more annoying
to a woman than being left to
    her own discretion. Mine waits
for me. Goodbye, my dear fellows, come
    back tomorrow, and perhaps
I shall get on a little with
    my chronicle of vanishings.
Burckhardt locates the psychic sources

of learning, of scholarship,
in "our unfulfilled longing for what
   has vanished"—let me say it
for you as well as he does, *unsere
   unerfüllte sehnsucht nach
dem Untergegangen* . . . So. You follow me,
   yes?
         We have been fortunate.
I really have enjoyed your visit—
   you must know: with you I seem
to hear myself speak as a stranger
   —without recognizing myself.
Only after you are gone shall I
   discover that it was . . . I.
Being alone is so important:
   you have to keep finding new
tactics for doing it—otherwise
   you feel at home so quickly,
which is to say you are quite lost.
                —No,
I shall not say any more:
my purpose henceforth will be to set
   words side by side in silence
and watch—watch the words.
            Goodbye, go now,
   leave me. Go. Goodbye, goodbye. . . .

A NOTE ABOUT THE AUTHOR

Richard Howard was born in 1929 in Cleveland, Ohio, and studied at Columbia University and the Sorbonne. After working for several years as a lexicographer, he became a translator from the French and has published over one hundred and fifty translations, including books by Gide, Giraudoux, Cocteau, Camus, DeBeauvoir, DeGaulle, Breton, Robbe-Grillet, Barthes, Cioran, Claude Simon and the complete *Les Fleurs du Mal* of Baudelaire, for which he received the American Book Award in translation. He is currently working on a new translation of Proust's *A la recherche du temps perdu*.

In 1970 he was awarded a Pulitzer Prize for his third book of poems, *Untitled Subjects*, and received the National Institute of Arts and Letters Literary Award for his books of poems up to that time; *Findings* (1972), *Two-Part Inventions* (1974), *Misgivings* (1979), and *Lining Up* (1984) followed.

His comprehensive critical study, *Alone with America: Essays on the Art of Poetry in the United States since 1950*, originally published in 1969, was reissued in an expanded edition with a new introduction in 1980. He is also the editor of *Preferences* (1974), a critical anthology. He has taught widely, reviewed widely, and received many honors for his work. In 1982 he was made a member of the American Institute and Academy of Arts and Letters. He lives in New York City.

A NOTE ON THE TYPE

This book was set in Monticello, a Linotype revival of the original Roman No. 1 cut by Archibald Binny and cast in 1796 by the Philadelphia type foundry Binny & Ronaldson. The face was named Monticello in honor of its use in the monumental fifty-volume *Papers of Thomas Jefferson*, published by Princeton University Press. Monticello is a transitional type design, embodying certain features of Bulmer and Baskerville, but it is a distinguished face in its own right.

Composition by Heritage Printers, Inc.,
Charlotte, North Carolina
Printed and bound by Halliday Lithographers,
West Hanover, Massachusetts
Designed by Harry Ford